TECHNIQUES & STRATEGIES:
TO INCREASE PARENT INVOLVEMENT

Techniques & Strategies: To Increase Parent Involvement

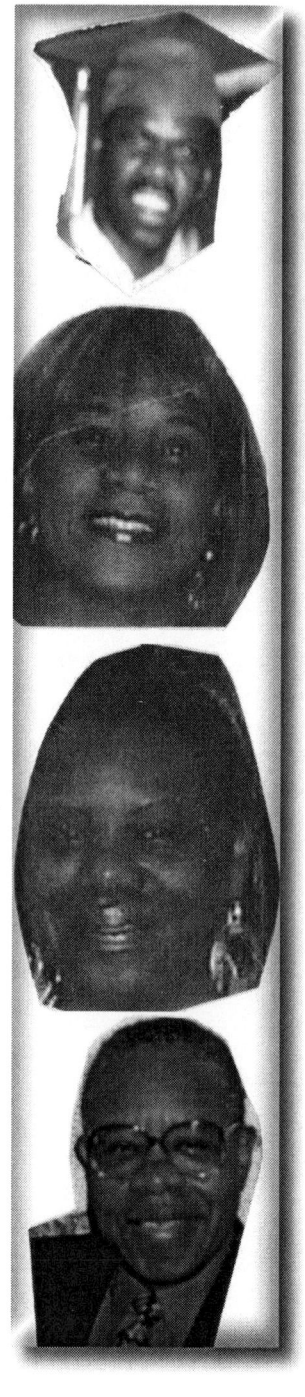

Give support to your children at home

When parents become involved, with their children's school, the commitment and dedication should be shared among the other siblings at home. This will probably become a necessary approach to continue to improve your children's academic achievements. If parents focus on this philosophy it strengthens support that each family sibling will appropriately participate in their school graduation.

Techniques & Strategies:
To Increase Parent Involvement

PARENT COMMUNITY
SCHOOL CONNECTIONS
COMMITTEE

Ann A. Brown

Copyright © 2012 by Ann A. Brown.

Library of Congress Control Number: 2012908338
ISBN: Softcover   978-1-4771-0450-7
                 Ebook   978-1-4771-0451-4

All rights reserved. No part of this book may be reproduced or transmitted in any form or by any means, electronic or mechanical, including photocopying, recording, or by any information storage and retrieval system, without permission in writing from the copyright owner.

This book was printed in the United States of America.

To order additional copies of this book, contact:
Xlibris Corporation
1-888-795-4274
www.Xlibris.com
Orders@Xlibris.com
113886

THE TABLE OF CONTENTS

Foreword 7
Preface: The process of developing the Parent Community
    Schools Connection Committee 9
Acknowledgments 11
Introduction 13
Chapter 1: The Importance of Parent Conferences 17
Chapter 2: The Beginning of Our Mission with the PCSCC 23
Chapter 3: Parents can make significant changes to improve
    their child's scores 31
Chapter 4: Little Zion Baptist Church 39
Chapter 5 41
Chapter 6 46
Chapter 7 52
Chapter 8 57
Chapter 9: Grading a Child is important 59
Chapter 10 62
References 65

Foreword

Dear Ann:

This letter is to affirm my earlier expression of support for the Parent Community School Connections Committee. It is widely recognized that parental involvement in the education process is a critical factor in children's success. It is also understood that for any number of reasons, unfortunately, many children do enjoy the benefit of such involvement. The PCSCC is committed to addressing that problematic situation.

Speaking as a retired University Administrator and Professor, I feel that developing a relationship between the teacher and the parent, could be the accomplishment which could enhance ongoing commitment. I can only welcome such a mission and thank you for your role in developing and spearheading the Committee's motivational effort.

As you well know, Williamsburg school system has committed itself to elimination of the so-called "achievement gap" between Majority and Minority students. This goal is as ambitious as it is worthy. WJC will need use every resource at its disposal if it hopes to succeed, and it cannot afford to fail. As WJC will need develops the specifics of this effort, I am sure the potential PCSCC concept offers will become increasingly evident.

Knowing the achievement gap remains a problem for both affected children and their parents today, it is both timely and appropriate that you can choose to write this book now. Parent involvement is being analyzed by many authors on a regular basis, but your experience offers unique insight in to this issue . . . I believe using the essential components of the kind of committee you propose in order to advocate and structure parental participation can be the key to their successful participation in their children's education.

In that regard, let me also thank you again for your distinguished service on the WJC County School Board and your continuing commitment to make public education better for all children.

> Sincerely,
> John Alewynse, PhD.

Preface

The process of developing the Parent Community Schools Connection Committee

The parent community schools connections committee, included parents, schools, and the community, that is our reason for choosing the name. This committee started in 2003 with the development of our mission. There were many things that had to be developed. The incorporation of all the components had to be connected into a package before we started our visiting of the ministers, schools, and recruiting parents to join. All the members wanted a clear picture of the process of developing a committee especially when you start from the beginning.

Parent involvement was an important issue, which was worthy to be discussed and studied. It should be done continually. Fortunately for me, our committee consisted of teachers, principals, parents, also some community persons that were interested in helping our cause. This group developed ideas and soon became a reality; we were ready to get started. Then we set up meeting with the community supports. All members met with the pastors, parents, schools, and the PTA. Notes from the PCSCC

I was hoping that writing this book will help individuals who are interested in parent involvement to do further studies. "Parent involvement will help to decrease the achievement gap between minority and majority students." Since my story is a true experience that happened to me, it could naturally become beneficial to other studies engaging parents in their child's education.

Hal Pashler, PhD, said "his research in cognitive psychology could help us understand and address common problems in teaching and learning." Dr. Pashler mentioned in his book titled Organizing Instruction and Study to Improve Student Learning that it was important to get parents involved. Dr. Pashler also pointed out a different premise about teacher participation with students. He also said, "Those teachers have to do more preparation in order to narrow the achievement gap. The best way to accomplish this would be recruiting parents in the classroom and give them activities to perform. Help them feel at ease being in the classroom. When parents are in the classroom a student's behavior and work habits changes for the better just because parents are present in the class."

National Standard for Parent/Family Involvement programs, which include parenting, student learning, volunteering, and student understanding in collaboration with the community, is the best reasoning to tackle this problem.

My actual story shows how I struggled to bring a group of people together as a committee with a notion that the construction of this group was the way to help children and parents to decrease the majority and minority gap in school achievement.

Acknowledgments

I am very appreciative and grateful to Willie Brown (my husband) for all the assistance he gave me. Willie worked, tirelessly by my side, he too believed in the mission adopted for our committee. Catherine Parker was one of the first to join our group. She displayed her dedication and commitment to get the committee up and running. Of course, I must thank my wonderful children Phyllis, Edward, and Renita for their moral support given to their mother. Special thanks to Joyce Huffman for her support and friendship. Also a thank you to BJ Lowenhaupt. Much of the information from the book she gave me was very helpful concerning parent involvement. Members were dedicated, dependable and volunteered to work with me on this important project. The committee consisted of Principals, Teachers, Pastors, Parents and interested people of our community. All of the members of the committee did a marvelous job persuading and encouraging parents to become engaged in the Williamsburg schools.

Many people had mentioned to us it was a long overdue assignment which should have been addressed long ago. Parents should start to visit their child's classroom and that was our great challenge to motivate parents to take a look at this problem. The mission must be successful. The Minority children needed all of the help possible from their parents and teachers. Parents would have to start visiting the classroom in order to close this minority gap.

Our committee had thoughts to visit and discuss our goals with the Pastors of the churches in the community. It was suggested to combine the collaboration of ideas concerning the PCSCC. After our first three meeting with them I knew we were on the correct track. The Principals, teachers and, Pastors, along with some of parents were willing to assist the Parent Committee. We had their permission to use their churches for our presentations. It was decided that we would rotate our events in the churches on a monthly basis.

The Pastors of the Baptist churches has demonstrated their kindness and dedication, along with cohesiveness to the committee, in this important cause and overwhelming support. I will never forget the WJCC School system to give permission our Parent Education meetings in their conference rooms at the schools.

One of my close friends, who has a MS in Communication Disorders, commented to me that parents, teachers and students, should have a relationship together. It makes the student excel in their achievements. Another, long time friend, Carlotta Hebblethwaite PhD. indicated that parent participation is a wonderful idea for student advancement.

<u>*Several names have been changed due to protecting confidentiality privileges.</u>

Introduction

The first contact I had with parent involvement happened to me at an early age; during my attendance in elementary school. My mom visited the school as often as possible. The two children at home were my older brother and me. Our parents were very hard working people who strongly believed in education for both of us. My mom was the parent that did most of the classroom visits at the school. My dad worked long hours to take care of his family. He would come to school for a special event such as a school play. You could be assured that my mother was definitely interested in building a relationship with the classroom teacher. Many other students would say to me, "my mom has not visited the school at anytime" Essentially mom being persistent with this exercise on a regular basis, this was a conformation that parent involvement is essential to academic achievement. She always explained to the teacher, if there is a need to call me do not hesitate.

Probably sub-consciously she appropriately showed dedication to parent involvement explained my interest. In time, I too participated in parent involvement in my children's classroom. I became a teacher aide. I was given the assignment to work with a pre-K program just like the class my younger daughter was attending. Married now with three children of my own, this tradition continued because every chance I had leads me to visit my children in their classroom and meet their teacher. It was a plus that this employment was under the Buffalo Board of Education this made it easier for me to make visits to my children's schools. Eventually, I was selected to become a Community Aide, which entailed making visits to homes of children that were in our program and try to empower the parents to come in and meet their child's teacher. This was a very enlighten duty for me due to my beliefs in parent engagement in the schools were very important for parents to be involved.

How I encouraged parents to come to my classroom

Over many years, it becomes second nature to work with parents about problems that their child may develop in the classroom. I thought about the time, that I went to some of the homes of my students.

Everything I tried, to get parents into the classroom was an inappropriate method. So one day after school I decided to visit some of my student's homes. It was important to assist the development of my student's achievements.

As I parked my car and went to the first home, the parent came to the door and immediately, we both spoke to each other. As we talked, I explained my dedicated interest to have her come to my class for a visit. Furthermore, as the communication became more engaged in a positive nature, we hugged and she promised to visit the classroom.

Just as I was leaving her home to go to another, several people came outside and started talking to us, as we made introductions, mental images started to develop in my mind about possible visits from other parents members.

It was very difficult to imagine or measure what actually happened. There were several people began to talk at the same time about coming to my classroom to see me.

This was over whelming experience, it was never expected that so many parents consented to come to the school. This was so great to realize that all I had to do was visit their homes to engage them to be involved. The next several days' parents came in and helped me with classroom activities. This parent visiting continued on a regular basis. Their objection to visiting the schools was the parents did not feel anyone really wanted them to become involved. An idea that came to me, that entailed me to put up a sign that said" Parents' Welcomed!" All I needed to do was add some chairs, a table, coffee, and treats. The parents liked my idea and on many occasions some would stay for a long period of time.

Making home visits, which did give me a positive perception to get parents to participate in the school activities, which was a tremendous support for my students and their effective academic improvements.

Table 1.

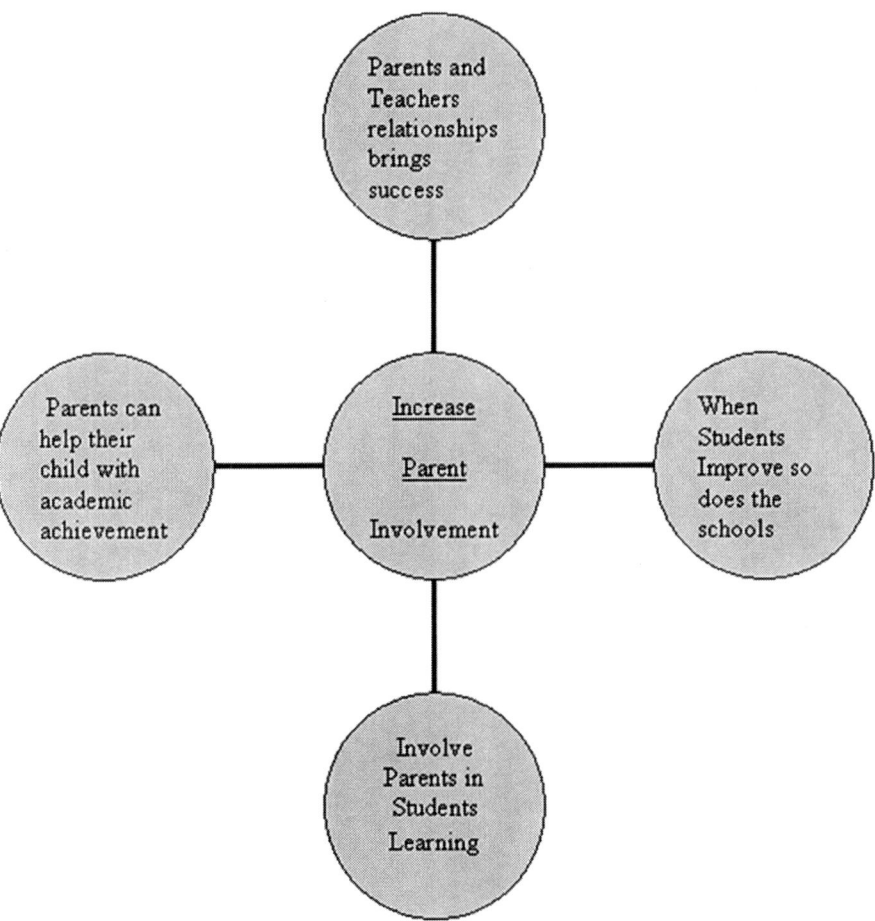

Chapter 1

The Importance of Parent Conferences

Before I start with the step-by-step development of the PCSCC, let us discuss parent-teacher conferences. Developing this particular commitment is favorable to have in any school. The Parent Community School Connections Committee will help you with all your thoughts and concerns, which are developed into this special conference. This conference is a great technique to combine all necessary questions that parents and teachers may need to know; it is possible to develop a good relationship between both individuals. This meeting involves the importance of your child, the school, the parent, and the child's learning situation.

This conference is one of the most essential parts of the relationship between parents and teachers. The Parent Community School Connections Committee (PCSCC) was influential, and it advocated for parents to get involved with the schools. Our group represents and actually fosters parent involvement and anyone who is a member of the student's family.

Additionally, teachers who may need to make a contact relationship or some kind of agreement with a parent has the opportunity to choose the activity at that time. It is essential for a parent with a teacher relationship to bloom. More importantly, it is an important conversation, which retrieves necessary information between both individuals.

> The Parent Community School Connections Committee has been in existence since 2003. The explicit mission revolved

around strengthening the parent-school community relationship in order to help close the minority achievement gap. Parental involvement plays a major role in educating their children. Most studies cite "how important a parent is in the maturation, human development, growth and academic achievement of their children" (local newspaper in Williamsburg, the Virginia Gazette)

But this philosophy is not all about making parents think there is no hope left. It is about understanding that parents must work harder in order to help their child. The time is too short; you, as a parent, have the responsibility to help. If you are a working parent, you can possibly set up a special classroom schedule to visit your child. I am hoping to give you the confidence that it can be done. There is so much you can teach your child at home just by going to the classroom and meeting their teacher. The more staff you meet at the school, the more you will learn about your child. When my children were in elementary and high school, I would visit their classes, sit down in class, and observe what takes place; this took place all through high school. I knew all the principals and most of the teachers; they also knew who I was. Once while visiting, I made a decision to eat my lunch in the cafeteria and chat with some of the staff. My children were in different schools; even though they were a good distance apart, it was my responsibility to talk with their teachers as it was the parent's duty to drive to each school and see their teacher. My objective was to give support to my children in any way that was appropriate. In my book, we will cover this subject often; there is never enough information distributed about the importance of building a relationship with your child's teacher. The schools should essentially give parents as much literature, with details concerning parents visiting, especially if it relates to being committed and involved with the child's academic achievement. This should come first. Taking a first step is an essential part, and it is the beginning of children's comprehension to excel in school.

During the time I was attending the (State University of Buffalo) my children would walk along with me. Everyday routines with your children really bring you closer to becoming a part of their everyday educational routine. On some occasions, one of them would attend my class with me, at the University, if it did not interfere with their school schedule.

In order for students to become encouraged and motivated about their classroom activities, let the parents build a rapport with the classroom teacher. If you think about it, your relationship with your child will improve continually.

Now you may have a better understanding about my strong analyst concerning parent participation. This is an important part of everything you stand for due to the importance of raising children. Be involved, establish a relationship with the teacher, visit the school often, and make notes if needed to develop, a day to day report with current information. If the parents came to their child's classroom, most of those negative effects would change completely over time.

As an elementary teacher, I was convinced that there was a purposeful way for children to make tremendous changes in their performance in the classroom with parent involvement. This technique was a great success getting parents involved. The exposure to parent recruitment helped me to encourage parental involvement and make it work. That approach is the key to my book that made a great difference in increasing parent involvement. More importantly, it developed to a group of professionals that volunteered to become members of this committee. Actually, this was the best way to assist parents to get involved. Together, we would find a way to encourage parents to visit their child's school. I realized this would be an ongoing process for all the members. I was willing and up to the challenge because this problem within the educational system should be dissolved. My reasoning for establishing a professional group like the Parent Community School Connections Committee would be beneficial to assisting in this matter and give every advantage to our parents. If any situation arises, the parents will come to us for assistance. Our members could find a way to solve the problem. It was a triumph for the committee; we didn't want any expression of disapproval to discourage them from attending the classroom. Obviously, my opportunity to accomplish this intensive motivation would soon develop into a parent involvement committee. This moment would be a great opportunity for all the members. There had never been a committee like this in the city before. In 2002, an opportunity developed that led me to enter an election within my district. My thoughts were, if I could win this seat on WJC School Board, this would assist me to be more helpful to the parent needs. Actually, not many people knew anything about me at first when I moved to WJCC, but the press gave me an interview and put it into the paper. My background in education made an over whelming difference to this community. Fortunately, the people of my district went to the polls, and voted for me. I won the seat for the WJC School Board which was a tremendous and proud accomplishment. So immediately I started the establishment of this partnership committee, which would help children to succeed with the help of their parents. Having this seat on the school board would give me a wider range to assist the parents and also work with some of the teachers and principals of the school system.

On my first board meeting, I spoke about this committee and how it could be an asset to assist the minority gap in education. There were many children that were failing on the SOL'S exams and also their classroom exams. The implications were centered specifically toward minorities' students. Majority students were performing in the higher brackets successfully. In essence, you still need to advocate for the minority children to bring about acceptable scores for everyone. If the minority children did not pass the exams, this also affected the majority students' progress. They too were at a standstill.

The main issue here is evaluated according to the No Child Left Behind Act, which is a U S government program. Theses minority students have to at least pass the (AYP—Average Yearly Passing Average) passing level. If they do not reach a total of 69% on these tests, the next step would be Probation status. All schools that fall under this category would be responsible to assist their students until the next tests are administered . . . Fortunately, they give a time period for the schools to improve their SOL'S scores. This process, of course, would find a way to reach the newspapers; and there will be a column in the local attractions for all to read. This situation was not a very joyous occasion for the city. More importantly, I recently found out this was a problematic situation for the WJC school system when I became a school board member. Some of the board members expressed that taking the lead to start this committee would give the school an advantage. This committee would put us on the right road to find the proper ways to reduce this gap. The school board members were pleased to help eliminate this problem. This dilemma was an inadequacy within the school system and a problem long before I arrived to Williamsburg James City County. I can personally work on this complex problem by starting the <u>Parent</u>

<u>Community School Connections Committee</u>. This mission was designed to focus on this very complex issue, and I had to get started recruiting and persuading parents to visit the schools. This was the part which was something that fit my personality—talking with people.

The PCSCC would explore this consideration with volunteers that will be working with me. We had to handle this essential situation and make it successful. More importantly, it would be influential for <u>establishing techniques and strategies for our goals, missions, and objectives</u>. The development of the PCSCC was essential to the success of the minority gap. This action would improve academic performance of those students. There was an article in our local newspaper about the SOL scores, which showed that the minority students scored lower than the majority students. (I would show this article to you a little later) It was the exact time to approach the establishing of this committee. Actually, there are many ways to assist this logically, but the group that would work with me would have to be successful because other people were depending on us.

As a school board member, you are responsible to visit all the schools in your district to introduce yourself. While performing this responsibility I spoke about the PCSCC, and which staff members would like to join. I happened to meet many people that had an interest in joining the committee. There was no need to waste time on this important matter. Several people from different schools volunteered to join in with me in this endeavor. These volunteers were able to find accommodations to get a conference room in a high school that was offered to us to have our meetings in. This kind gesture was promoted by the principal of the school. It was just wonderful to see this process was falling into place with this new group. I set up a meeting for all the volunteers from several schools as soon as possible. We started with a membership of seven people, which included as follows: two principals, four teachers, and one parent. The commitment of seven people to join the group was sufficient to share their ideas as to what policies we would probably incorporate into our mission statement. I was very grateful to have so many people from the school staff to be committed to helping our parents to become involved.

Actually this was the final stage to our establishment: *the Parent Community School Connections Committee.*

The idea behind the name was to include different aspects dealing with education. I developed this committee specifically to bring the parents, community, school, and children connected together under one umbrella. The committee would be able to contribute procedures that would lead to success. Since all our members were very familiar with the WJC school system, just that attribute alone would be beneficial.

Chapter 2

The Beginning of Our Mission with the PCSCC

Preadmissions for our Mission Statement

- Visit the churches in the community and introduce our committee members.
- Recruit parents from the churches and community.
- Present agreements with the ministers (also pinpoint exactly the problems of parent members at the church).
- Gain the support of the ministers on board to assist PCSCC. (Many of the parents attended most of these Baptist churches in the community. So it is obvious to have these events there. Sometimes you have to go to the parents and explain why it is important for this committee also what our members planned to recommend for the parents to be inspired. They deserve a full explanation of our intentions.
- Have the confirmation of the ministers when we can start having parents' workshops, parents' forums, parent/education meetings and have the approval to conduct each event at their churches. These pastors have decided to join in with the Parent Community School Connections Committee.
- Have meetings with the administration, principals, and teachers of the WJC schools. We will set up these events in the schools too.

- Inform parents about conducting the parent/education meeting, parents' forums, and parents' workshops also in a different setting from the church and schools if the possibility presents itself.
- Conduct a meeting with the PTA and inform the members of our mission with the schools.
- Start setting up dates for the forums, workshops, and parent/education meetings.
- Vote on information collected from all the community and set up our missions, objectives, and goals for the Parent Community Schools Connections Committee. (Our first task was to combine our pergolas work together in to our mission statement. During this stage, we had to construct our plan of operation [year 2003]. So once the mission statement was completed we actually started to administer our mission, which began by visiting and talking to people in the community.)

The Completed Mission Statement

1. Close the achievement gap between minority and majority students.

2. Foster and enhance parent-school relationships.

3. Communicate the established mission and objectives of the committee through outreach opportunities with parents and other community stakeholders.

4. Establish public forums and workshops to gather information from and to enhance communication with parents and other community stakeholders.

5. At the end of each year, start recommendations on how to move ahead with parent involvement ideas and new strategies.

6. Identify committee activities and evaluate them also and take a close look at our annual progress.

Objectives

1. Build relationships within the larger community that will foster the development of a culture that will support parent efforts to become more engaged in the education of their children.

2. Serve as a catalyst to encourage more parental involvement in the schools.

3. Identify and characterize effective entities and individuals who bridge barriers to parent involvement.

4. Serve in a multidimensional capacity to facilitate the creation of a community attitude that values, encourages, and embraces the rightful place of parents, caregivers, and adoptive parents.

5. Have the chair assign each member of our committee to be liaisons with all the pastors that are working directly with PCSCC. Each member is assigned with one pastor. Having appointed these liaisons, each person will establish the opportunity to work together on different projects with the pastors. Specifically, have ongoing recruitments of more parents to attend parents' workshops and forums that will be conducted at the churches by our committee. The school membership and the pastors would send out memos about the events, which the committees would conduct at their facility. Either the school or church will send out correspondence to everyone about the time and place for this affair.

Goals

1. Conduct parents' workshops and forums that will bring parents to meet PCSCC.
2. Identify target sites to conduct these events.

3. Meet with the pastors in the community and set up PCSCC events at the targeted sites.

4. Close the achievement gap between minority and majority students.

5. Foster/enhance parent-school relationships.

6. Presentations given by our members with information that was necessary for parents.

7. Review related literature that will give our committee more incite and updates on parent involvement programs.

8. Share our procedures and progresses with the entire school system by mailing out the information on a regular basis.

9. Conduct regular meetings at other schools in the community to share information and solicit ideas from other school staff.

10. Set up events for parents with some of the schools.

Here is an example of some communication sent to a few of our pastors. It explains what events are planned for their church.

Dear Pastor:

Parent Community School Connections Committee will schedule a parents' forum at the Chickhominy Baptist Church, on Wednesday, January 18, 2005, at 6:00 PM. Members will discuss several different topics that will be of benefit to your parents and other interested people from your community. First, we will spend some time getting acquainted with your congregation. Our members were assigned specific topics to present at the parents' forums. We will also have some snacks for attendees. Here are the topics for this program:

Introduction—Ann Brown

Purpose of the PCSCC—Willie Brown

Discussion on the best way to get parents involved in the schools.—Catherine Parker

SOL'S, Graduation requirements, and available resources—Mr. Ranch and Mr. Gray Summary—Mr. Edwin

Questions and answers—Willie Brown

We are very appreciative to the pastor and congregation for their support with the PCSCC.

Sincerely,

Ann Brown
—Chair

The school system administration answered all questions for our parents. Here are the questions. Many parents have concerns about the school system, and at best, it is strongly considerable to have these answers so quickly.

Q.

1. When is the appropriate time for teachers to notify a parent that their child is failing in order to assist with the student's SOL status?

A.

It is recommended that elementary and middle school teachers notify parents as soon as they know. Teachers are able to observe when student is expecting difficulty at school. They are able to suggest what can be done in the classroom and give parents helpful tips for working with students in their homes. Parents should remember that passing a course and passing the SOL test are two different matters. Students at the high school level should share their graded work with parents daily. This information should also indicate and goal setting. Parents should also be aware of the dates for interim report marking periods.

Q.

2. Minority parents are still saying that they do not feel welcome in the school community. What can be done to improve this situation?

A.

Providing culturally sensitive schools is a plan in WJCC schools. We support parents in their efforts to have happy, well-adjusted, and successful children. Oftentimes, parents may recall their own unpleasant experiences while attending school. We recommend that parents pursue the communication with the classroom teachers to discuss immediate concerns. Unresolved concerns should be directed to the school principal. The school principal can fulfill his or her duties if parents contact the main office to request appointments to discuss crucial matters.

Q.

What can the school system do to help get more parents involved in the schools, and can there be a questionnaire sent to teachers to fill out this topic?

A.

Each WJCC school has an active parent teachers association. The PTA council for our school system maintains monthly outreach to solicit parent involvement. The president of your child's PTA will be glad to speak to you. Parents are encouraged to volunteer and to attend scheduled programs and activities. Feel free to ask the principal directly how you can be more involved.

Q.

If students need more help with their classroom performance, can the schools set a certain amount of hours a week to work with their students directly and on a one-on-one basis? Can this be continued until progress is evident?

A.

After-school tutorials are provided for students "of need" or "with promise." Some schools also provide early morning tutoring and lunch tutorials as well. Mentoring is another important opportunity for students to receive help from teachers one student at a time. James River Elementary has a Saturday academy and Toano middle school hosts the Rites of Passage Program on Saturday morning.

Q.

5. I have a child that is enrolled in the alternative school. What will happen since the hours are changing?

A.

The matter regarding the alternative school is ongoing. Final details for the next school year will be forthcoming.

Q.

6. Parents are also concerned about their children that are placed in the special education program. They are saying that many students are placed in special education too soon. Is any monitoring done on this list of students that are being placed in special education?

A.

Yes. Our school system has joined other school divisions throughout the commonwealth in developing an action plan to reduce disproportional. We acknowledge that there is a disproportionate representation of African American students in special education programs. The Office of Student Services will provide professional development to teachers on how to interact and teach in culturally diverse environments. Parents should continue to advocate for their children by attending all scheduled child study meetings. If you need to talk with someone about this subject, contact the special education supervisor and get more information on this matter.

Parent/Education Committee Meeting

Parent/educational meeting—the PCSCC membership will make a presentation to the congregation at a Sunday morning service at the Historical First Baptist Church. We will enlighten everyone about what the PCSCC stands for and how important it is for parents to be involved with our committee and help to work with their child at home and in the classroom

Dear Pastor:

This letter is to let you know that the Parent Community School Connections Committee will be visiting Historical First Baptist Church on Sunday, January 8, 2006. Our group plans to speak to the congregation about the purpose of the PCSCC and how attending your church would assist us tremendously with elevating our rapport with your parents.

The committee is constantly building our relationship parents to get them to visit their child's school. Parents' coming in to the classroom to meet the teacher is the best way to help their child's academic achievement.

Thank you so much for working with our committee. We will be looking forward to seeing you and the congregation on that particular Sunday at 11:00 a.m.

Sincerely,

Ann Brown
Chair

Chapter 3

Parents can make significant changes to improve their child's scores

The PCSCC tries to break down those barriers and concerns into positive possibilities. Our committee encourages parents to visit their child's school by explaining to parents that their child needs help now. Those children who were failing are basically the minority and poor students, according to the schools' data. But the PCSCC had the opportunity to actually see the data from the school system. Therefore, parents have to make significant changes to improve their child's scores. The parents must meet their child's teacher immediately and build a relationship that hopefully will be a lasting one. This is why our committee tries so hard to get the parents involved and have forums to explain why they help their children to excel in their scores and to make a relationship with the child's teacher. The committee intends to be successful in establishing many different techniques that will assist the underlying ongoing problem of parent involvement.

During the course of this committee, in order to give consistency to our efforts, parent involvement should be a part of their child's classroom; this information will be repeated or mentioned often all through this book. This is one of our strategies, *be redundant* and *stress the importance* of this situation until all parents realize how important this is to their child.

In order for the child to improve, the parent has to be involved. The more staff you know, the more informed you are about your child's progress. I repeat, you should volunteer to help with activities in the classrooms.

I cannot explain this enough. You can help the teacher with classroom activities and be a part of the child's education all at the same time. Sign up for assisting the teacher at least once a week and develop a regular routine. It is important to continue to show interest if you want success because it will be helpful to your child's future. Make sure that you also attend the parent-teacher conferences and look into becoming a member of the parent-teachers organization. Both of these important events are influential to promoting success. The committee gives reminders to parents at each workshop, forum, or educational meetings, which will provide support for each of them, and also different information that helps keep them updated.

If the PCSCC plans on being successful and if this has given teachers the opportunity to make adjustments in their classrooms to accommodate this strategic plan, we must address the effects of the achievement gap. It would be beneficial to everyone. This could help close the achievement gap for minority's students. Parents and teachers must work together. This predicament can only change if parents work with PCSCC and the schools.

Always be aware of the probability for success if you try a different plan that may be successful for the students. Even though I must admit that new strategies do not always work for every child, but never give up the possibility it may be remarkably successful.

The PCSCC parents' assistance is to help this possibility to be a reality. Many of our parents have mentioned programs that would help them in finding the right books for their children to read at home. Parents try very hard to find the right materials and how they will use them with the children. All parents must read with and to their child or children.

These programs must be available to train parents that have concerns of having a help guide that will be particularly useful reading in certain areas. This material will be introduced to our committee members at our next PCSCC meeting, and we will discuss the possibilities to pursue and make a connection with this kind of family program and find a way to get students and parents involved. There are many organizations in our community that provide extra-purposeful educational help for our parents, and on many occasions, we share those academic support groups with our parents. Most of these programs are after school and even on Saturdays. Our school system also has several reading and math programs conducted at many of the schools. A few of our parents are attending these programs with their child. These types of programs are appropriate for our parents and their children also. We do make referrals for this kind of support if needed.

If parents do visit their child's classroom, listen to their suggestions and maybe put those ideas on your bulletin board. This will let the parents know that they are needed in the classroom and for them to feel proud. Parents visiting their child's classroom with the teacher could be the greatest part of your day. One important point to remember is student behavior is usually better with the parent in the classroom. This I know was a very beneficial personal experience for me.

Table 1. These list is the total parents 'that attended our Parent workshops and Parent forums.

The years that were included in these totals range 2004-2007

WJCC Schools	Parents That Attended
1. Berkeley MS	28
2. Lafayette HS	57
3. James River ES	36
4. James Blair MS	55
5. Stonehouse ES	06
6. Toano MS	54

WJCC Churches/Other Events

1. Bethel Restoration Center (first meeting)	26

2. Chickahominy Baptist Church	60
3. New Zion Baptist (first educational meeting)	15
4. Mount Pleasant Baptist Church (first meeting)	17
5. Grove Area Picnic Day	70
6. NAACP Youth Group (presentation only, we spoke to the youth)	
7. Bethel Restoration Center (Parent meeting with PCSCC)	125

WJCC Churches

1. New Zion Baptist—second meeting (parents' workshop)	65
2. Little Zion Baptist	17
3. Historical First Baptist (Sunday church service)	200
4. Mount Pleasant Baptist (second meeting)	12

888 Total Parents attended

We gave parents surveys during this special parent events conducted by the PCSCC; we looked at their concerns about their child's educational performance. They visited the classroom, got involved with classroom activities, and met the teacher.

Examining the essential information, this documented total of parents that attended our events was astonishing and extraordinary. The group was not assured this possibility would particularly motivate parents to be a part of the PCSCC-constructed group, but the information showed points out that we influenced the parent to be a part of their child's education.

Our recruitment procedures worked because the parents felt we were there to assist them and give guidance and support when needed. This was perhaps why during the course of our committee, we had parents that joined our membership, which I thought was essential. The parents enjoyed working with us and mentioned many times that our committee was very supportive to the parents and that they felt comfortable.

All of us worked as a team and our effort to supply our parents with the correct information to their questions at our constructed events. More importantly, our relationships with parents were specifically enriching and influential and should be acknowledged as instrumental to school relations. In my opinion, this committee has showed concern and commitment.

Table 2.

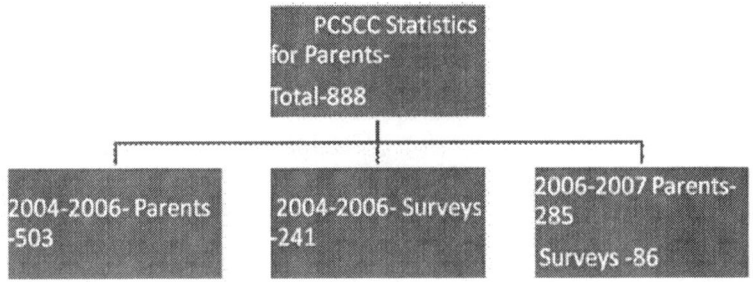

PCSCC has a meeting with the PTA

The president of the elementary school's PTA invited the Parent Community School Connections Committee to conduct a presentation at their PTA meeting. We talked to the members about the purpose of the PCSCC and explained how our group had expanded with more members to join our committee. It is essential to keep trying to identify parents to get involved. Each member had special information to present. Most of the PTA members mentioned that PCSCC does empower parents to visit the schools and meet the child's teacher. They assured us that if we needed any additional help, that we just contact their office.

Most importantly, the PTA advocates for parents and assists them with services that are requested for parental help. The PTA group was advocating that we conduct a parents' workshop at their school at a later date. I explained to this group that we would make arrangements to set up a date to conduct this event. These dedicated ladies were very supportive about our work in assisting minority parents. This particular group had very few minority students, but ultimately, they were motivated to assist us in every way possible, even to conduct an event to persuade parents to join our group. They also mentioned that the population may change at some time in the future. So then we would be aware of what could take place and how the situation could be helped.

The president of the PTA acknowledged to the group that she wanted to present a particular book that would give support to our approach of recruiting parents. This book examined how parents have to be committed in order to help their child with academic achievement. I was overwhelmed and grateful with the consideration to give our committee this wonderful book.

The PTA is essential to working with parents. They are motivated and dedicated to help all parents with different kinds of problems or situations that happen in schools.

Tips for Parents to Stay Involved with Their Child's Education

Our committee is always continually illustrating the importance of being involved in your child's classroom.

1. Visit the schools; get a school schedule and calendar.
2. Make sure children start strong with a healthy breakfast.
3. Make a record; give your child a notebook and make sure you check if they are writing school information in it.
4. Set a study time, a quiet place, and a dedicated time to do homework.
5. Parents help your child to manage their time wisely.

Not Just another Pre-K Program (The Early Steps Program was a federally funded until about six years ago

Most of our concentration has been communicating concerns of parent involvement geared for elementary and the middle schools, but early education is definitely necessary to recruit parent involvement. Parents should be engaged and encouraged to visit the classroom of their child when they first enter a pre-K program.

According to many individuals, the Early Steps pre-kindergarten program are designed to provide disadvantaged children with experiences vital to later educational success. This program was also enhanced by parent involvement.

This may lead to a possible conclusion that if students do not enter programs like Early Steps and Early Push, they will have the same academic problems of achievements in elementary and middle school, and maybe in high school. These claims have been cited by some researchers.

The concept grows about kindergarten children that are minority and Hispanics that enter this grade level with a lack of skills. They perform far behind white students that attend kindergarten. Sometimes we may think that academic achievement relates to only elementary and middle school minority students, but kindergarten and pre-K are an important part of students excelling especially with the help of parent involvement.

This information gives the indication of how important it is to continue having parents involved in their child's education. I have a personal connection to the another program call Early Push. I worked there as a teacher aide and a community aide; it was one of my first paraprofessional jobs. Our program had a positive message for our parents—they could have lunch with their children, go on field trips together, and take neighborhood walks with their child, teacher, and teacher aide.

This kind of program was a different experience, one that would help the teacher accomplish her classroom goals. This parent visit could be continued for the entire day. Parent involvement participation was always at its highest in the Early Push Program.

Some of the teaching strategies picked out the target area—concept-building, improving of perception, verbal communication, and Peabody Picture Vocabulary testing. The teacher and I were a part of all mutual practices and testing in the classroom. These concepts were excellent in academic achievement in Early Push.

Chapter 4

Little Zion Baptist Church

PCSCC had a workshop at the Little Zion Baptist Church on May 5, 2007. Sessions topics and presenters

   a. SOL elementary and secondary—Mr. Gray
   b. Parent involvement the big picture—Catherine Parker
   c. Communication being a two-way process—Mr. Brooks
   d. Suggestions to discipline children—school and home—Ann and Willie Brown

The people that attended the workshop totaled twenty-one. There were {fifteen parents,} {two grandparents} and {four children}.

They filled out eleven surveys that contained all the questions and concerns. They all were collected and reviewed and answered at the workshop from members of the Committee.

<u>James City Schools had low test scores from Minority Students</u>

<u>These scores from the Minorities are not meeting the Federal Guide Lines</u>

James City___Chronic low test scores among African Americans, the Disable and the Poor Lead to only 4 of 12 WJC schools are meeting federal objectives based on SOL results released Tuesday. The results are preliminary scores. The problem is especially in the subject of math. The Federal Standards under **No Child Left Behind shortcomings among**

minorities. This is **the fourth straight year the division has failed** to meet the mandates set **by No Child Left Behind Minority,** for disabled and poor children. **The overall students, easily exceeding minimum standards for English and math at the elementary, middle and high school levels.**

NO CHILD LEFT BEHIND divides student among seven groups, among them whites, Hispanics and those with limited English proficiency. Blacks, the disabled and the poor all fell below the **English and math pass benchmarks of 69% and 67%** respectively. English scores were within a few point of passing, but math scores fell short by double digits and were 18 points short among disabled students. By contrast, Hispanics students scored 74.6%in English and 72% in math. The standards, known as an Annual Measurement **Objective, continually gets tougher. (Williamsburg Virginia Gazette Newspaper, 2005)**

Chapter 5

The PCSCC compared these scores from our minority students, and it indicated that our community has to continually persuade and recruit more parents to become engaged with their child's education.

It is the only way for minority students to progress in their academic achievements.

We want these students to excel in order to decrease the minority achievement gap. We, as a group, have to be persistent to recruit parents and make them understand the importance of parent involvement and visit the classroom and work with their child's teacher regularly.

In schools with poor and minority students, the levels of involvement should be consistent. Parents of children that have low achievement scores that are failing should be involved in their child's classroom, joining the PTA and having a discussion with the teacher. Compared with peers whose parents had high levels of school involvement, children with involved parents have a higher academic achievement. Building a relationship between parents and teachers could help the vision of the school and change the academic achievement of these particular students. Actually, an agreement should be made between teacher, parent, and child.

Information for the Parents

Communication with your child is important and must be often. Discuss the things that occurred that day in the classroom. The child should keep notes of the activities in a notebook; parents can check it daily. Parents must listen to the teacher if it is reported that their child is failing. Then work with the teacher and visit regularly to keep up with the progress of your child.

Keep this information written down and provide a guide of how your child is adapting to the strategies that the teacher has been working with your child. Be firm with your child to keep on the right track. Just don't get angry because that does not assist with the problem. Give supporting words to help your child to adjust.

Parents are so important to the process of their child's increase in achievement scores; they must be reminded, and you must keep reminding them. When we had our events at the church, schools, or other community places, it was a breathtaking moment because so many parents were ready to listen as to their being an important factor in their child's life.

Without your parent involvement, your child will not continue to progress. Classroom visits keeps you informed about your child, and there is nothing that would contribute to success more than seeing it for yourself. Then you can ask questions, make comments, observe, and get updates on how your child is performing in the classroom (PCSCC notes).

Many times I have spoken to parents in a private conversation concerning these matters. We do respect the confidentially contract just like the WJC schools.

A parent was rather disheartened about how her child was performing in class. I assured her if she communicated with the teacher and find out what the problem was, then both of them could find a solution together. The members of the committee are capable of discussing with parents and assisting them with any kind of problem. But we must respect their privacy.

Many of the parents have called us on the phone, and since I was a school board member, I would call the principal or teacher and share the parent's concern, and usually the problem would be resolved the next day. The principal would call me with the results of their consultations, and in turn, I passed it along to the parent. Another incident happened; a grandmother contacted me. In turn, I made a call to the principal, and we talked, and this situation was no longer a problem. Each time I had to discuss problems with the school staff; regardless my appreciation was always shared with them.

My Relationship with Parents Helped the Performance of Students in My Classroom

When I was an elementary teacher, often, parents would just visit my classroom to relax and talk with me. I put my schedule for parents on the bulletin board where it was displayed to information parents. Occasionally, the principal would allow me extra time to communicate with parents if there was a problem or a serious matter. Sometimes, the parent and I had lunch in my classroom to talk. The important idea was to let them know you care about them! These methods worked for me.

To enhance my relationship with parents, if they needed to communicate a longer period, I would accommodate that parent. Never let a parent leave without discussing their problem. Parents that wanted to remain in my classroom would sit down and stay while I was teaching the children. It was just great!

Sometimes they would ask me questions about a subject that made me feel the parents were comfortable with our relationship. I would just answer the question and continue with the lesson. Most teachers on our staff would not promote what specifically happened in my class, but for me, I encouraged this action. Ultimately, the rewards for this parent involvement would eventually help the children.

Parent Community School Connections Committee assists in building a partnership.

The PCSCC tries to break down those barriers and concerns at workshops/forums.

The group tries to encourage parents to visit their child's teacher right away.

If necessary, I would accompany the parent to the classroom only to reassure how important it is to visit and meet the teacher.

Your child deserves a good education, the way for that to happen is to visit the classroom.

For your child to receive a good education, parents have to be involved in the school.

But there is an option that I can accompany the parent if it makes them feel more comfortable.

Parents have that option to choose and we will support your choice (PCSCC notes).

The committee's mission is to work diligently to engage parents to realize the importance of meeting the classroom teacher now and signing a contract as soon as possible with the teacher.

Here are more questions and answers to share with our parents. We appreciate the administration of the schools for answering our parents' questions; it means a great deal.

Q. I am worried about the academic progress of my child.
A. What I will suggest to you is to speak to your child's teacher, school administrator, or the school's guidance counselor. Sometimes it is good idea to inform the teacher in writing if you are busy working and can't get to the school.
Q. Where will I get the school supplies for the first day of school? Which products do the children need?
A. School supplies may be found at Target, Staples, and Wal-Mart stores. You can also find this information in the school's main office.
Q. Where can I get the necessary resources that are needed by my child?
A. You can make referrals for child study, teacher referral, or a 504 if you need help. Whatever you request always let your child's teacher know which one you decide. Just remember if your child has a child study, there is a possibility that it could lead to a special education referral.
Q. Is it possible to get a tutor for my child?
A. Yes. The school has a remedial program. The parent and the teacher will have to pinpoint and find out where exactly the problem is. Then the student will be referred by the teacher.

The main thought of those children's academic problem is disengaged parents. Parents should stay involved especially when the students get older. Do not give up on your child. Maybe if the school has a social worker that can visit some of the homes and speak to parents to try and persuade them to visit the school.

Parents have to be involved with the teacher. Maybe you can get the parent, student, and the teacher to sign a contract. Try to call some of the parents on the phone, but you cannot give up trying. If the students lack skills, make a parent contact immediately. This the only way for the child's success, especially in a case like this one, where in you want to close the minority achievement gap (PCSCC notes).

Our committee tries to enhance the relationship between parents, teachers, and the community. At some point, parents will be able to notice that people really care, and that when they build relations, usually it helps them to communicate with the teacher, and it helps their child at the same time.

Chapter 6

PCSCC will make presentations to targeted audiences with this dialogue:

It is done for the betterment of the child; also, we must work to keep parents to stay involved.

- Advertise in the local newspaper (Williamsburg local news).
- Post flyers in public and also in electronic media outlets also web pages.
- Keep planning events for parents to attend and to listen to appropriate educational experts.
- Take a look at more studies concerning the parent involvement approach as a positive step.
- Start recruiting new churches and incorporate more pastors to join PCSCC for the upcoming year.
- Keep an ongoing list of new stakeholders in our strategic plan.
- Identify and attend venues that will also assist in soliciting parent inputs, such as church factions, Sunday morning services, back-to-school night, parent-teachers meetings, Grandparents' Day, and other community events.
- Cultural differences are both valid and valuable to discuss in a parent meeting.

Some parents of the PCSCC were not involved with very many teachers of the WJC school system at one time. Some parents have mentioned they feel somewhat uncomfortable, but when a parent comes in to meet their child's teacher, help them to be comfortable. Parents filled out many surveys at our parents' workshop at the New Zion Baptist Church. The event was attended by sixty-five parents. There was so much accomplished at the parents' workshop. Parents and other visitors were pleased about the sessions that were presented to them. Many parents mentioned that they want to be informed about when the next parents' workshop or event will take place.

A Message from a Parent School Volunteer

A parent was very disappointed about the school not being able to buy some new equipment. The parent wanted some new equipment in the school her child attended. The administration did not have the finances to obtain this equipment. The whole school knew the equipment was needed, but I guess the staff realized there was no funding to make a purchase, so it was a complicated situation.

Well, this parent did not give up! Everyone that the parent spoke with knew the problem that was occurring in her child's school. Regardless of what the administration said, that parent continued her negotiation with whoever would talk to her about this problem. On several occasions, the parent mentioned, "This is not just for my child, but for the good of all the children in this school." Little did I know that the next place the parent would visit to try and settle this dilemma was the WJC School Board?

I was chair of the school board and had been elected two years prior. The parent signed up to speak to the members of the school board. The complete details of the problem was described to the board. I explained to the parent that the school board's budget at that time did not have any extra funds allotted for any school. We did arrange a meeting at the school with the parent and superintendent to discuss the matter further. When I arrived, we took a tour of the school along with the principal. After the tour, everyone sat in on this emergency meeting we had with the parent about the funds for the new equipment.

Ethically the way this problem was handled was the proper approach to follow. Take a look at the school and examine the actual room and what equipment was needed also what makes this an essential problem to be negotiated for this school.

After the meeting finally ended, it was discovered that the equipment was desperately needed. So because of the parent's concern and dedication for the needs of the students, the additional materials would be bought and delivered into the classroom immediately.

Here is an example of a dedicated parent who decided to advocate for the students in order for the school to purchase some new equipment for a classroom.

All the school officials and school board members had a meeting to discuss the essential consideration of purchasing this equipment. The results of the meeting were influential toward the purchase of the new equipment. The parent was correct in her assumptions. As the chair of the school board, I suggested that we should look at our school budget once again and try and find money to buy at least some of this equipment. As I looked in the classroom, there wasn't any equipment to have a class. This room was not useable without any kind of equipment. To teach this subject, this equipment was necessary. It was understandable for everyone to try and overlook the fact of cost in this dilemma, but the students were not participating in the assigned class. Sometimes you have to make exceptions to the rule. The superintendent did an intensive search and found money to use for this project, but it was not the full amount of funds needed. I thought whatever amount it was, at least, the school would get some equipment. This parent was happy about our decision.

Parents are an important entity for the survival of the schools. We need parents' input on many situations, particularly in our school systems. If this parent had not been persistent and ethical in the acknowledgement of this absent equipment, it could have caused a difficult situation.

More importantly, we are very appreciative to have parent volunteers in our schools. There was obviously after what took place, and the effects of the impact of this situation could have been a big disappointment for our children. This also shows evidence that parents is a part of many aspects of education.

Having parents involved also helps them to learn more about how the school's operations work.

More importantly, parents are able to increase their understanding of what child development means if their presence is known. It is particularly beneficial to all students concerned with parent participation.

The parents actually observe what exactly happens in their child's classroom. This parent accomplished a remarkable discovery by this parent. She assisted the other students, and probably she to get equipment needed for this classroom. Thanks to this parent for being consistent in her dedication to the school.

Updated Mission for the PCSCC for 2007-2008

- The Parent Community School Connections Committee will continue to focus on strengthening the parent-school-community relationship in order to help close the minority achievement gap and continuing to conduct parents' forums and parents' workshops.
- Parent education in the churches and community venues to discuss any problems or concerns that parents may have.

Mission Strategies

- Close the achievement gap between minorities and majority students.
- Foster/enhance parent-school relationships.
- Communicate the established mission and objectives of the committee through continued outreach opportunities with area constituencies.
- Establish public forums and parents' workshops to gather information and to enhance communication with parents and other community stakeholders.
- Identify committee activities and annual accomplishments.
- Have a meeting with teachers who are having a very difficult time getting parents in their classroom. Our committee will set up regular communications with these teachers and observe if the group can give support and help talk with the named parents. Since we are a part of the school system, perhaps we could pursue reasons for this lack of cooperation.

Goals

- Build relationships with the larger community that will foster the development of a culture that will support parent efforts to become more engaged in the education of their children.
- Serve in a multidimensional capacity to facilitate the creation of a community attitude that values, encourages, and embraces the rightful place of parents, caregivers, and families in the education of their children.
- Serve as a catalyst to encourage more parental involvement in the schooling of children,

Objectives

- Use survey information to guide committee activities.
- Identify and characterize effective entities and individuals who can bridge barriers of parent involvement.
- Submit (at the end of the year) recommendation documents to the necessary and identified school officials and the school board.

Strategies/Actions Schedule (Ongoing)

- Publicize and promote the mission, objectives, and goals of the committee, both formally and informally, through various channels.
- Have planned and impromptu person-to-person discussions.
- Register the committee to the judicial and administration offices of Williamsburg, James City County.
- Make public presentation to targeted audiences.
- Continue conducting presentations at the community churches and schools.
- Sponsor, cosponsor, organize, facilitate, and attend forums, workshops, and other community events as opportunities arise; invite and prepare appropriate educational participants in the forums, workshops, and parents' meetings; stakeholders include but are not limited to parents, church pastors, school principals, PTAs, social services agencies, business leaders, teachers,

- Solicit, draft, and approve agenda items in advance for meeting, forums, and workshop.

*This document is solely for the use of the Parent Community School Connections Committee as registered in the James City County Office, Virginia.

Chapter 7

PCSCC Quick Facts

- Established in 2003
- Committee membership is voluntary
- Meeting on the second Monday of the month
- Schedule of meeting 4:00-5:30 p.m.
- Location of meeting is Lafayette High School
- Two-year Strategic Plan guides our activities
- Strategies include listening to parents, discussing concerns, and problem solving with the parents, schools, and other stakeholders.
- Methods: forums and parent feedback surveys
- Over 327 parent surveys collected to date
- Connections: churches (conducted events for parents in about nine churches so far)
- Connections: schools (conducted events for parents in about seven schools so far)
- Core message: Parent involvement has a positive effect on student achievement.
- Original documents: parent involvement flyer, *Parent Tips: How to Navigate a School* brochure and *what's in a Grade?* flyer
- Other information that is given to us by others is shared with the parents also.

Figure 4. **Here is a form filled out by our parents. The number on the line is the total number of parents who checked the particular category.**

Parents, please check each issue you would like to discuss for next year's events.

    __20__ Standards of learning (SOL)
    __12__ How the SOL affects a child's grade
    __15__ Graduation requirements
    __9__ Dress code, transportation, or attendance
    __25__ Being a parent volunteer at the school
    __17__ Assisting of the child with homework
    __30__ Building of a relationship between parents and the schools
    __11__ Parents being ready to make a contract with the classroom teacher
    __10__ Joining of the PTA
    __100__ Parents visiting the classroom last school year
    __14__ Concerns about being involved at the schools
    __4__ Other comments (A parent requested to have more parents' workshops next year. It was mentioned that parents could move around more and attend each session to collect more information.)

Name (Optional) _____

All right reserved. Materials belong to the PCSCC, a registered organization at the Clerk's Office of James City County, Virginia.

Williamsburg James City County Schools gave our committee the updates on academic assistance at the elementary level to update PCSCC.

- Daily reading and recovery programs to identify fourth grade students.
- Daily reading renewal support or students identified through PAT testing for Kindergarten through third and fifth grade.
- The after school program helps fourth and fifth graders that did not pass the reading or math SOL'S.
- Summer school for students who did not pass math or reading Sols
- Class-based support

Ways to Encourage Parents to Work with Their Child

1. Encourage parents to be involved by working with their child.
2. Remind parents of the positive effect of parent involvement on student achievement in school.
3. Help parents to be aware of their child's needs. This can mean to help in any way with homework, conference with the teachers, and reading to their child.
4. Encourage parents to visit their child's school to meet teachers, the principal, and other staff.
5. Help parents understand how schools work.
6. Provide special presentations to parents regarding topics such as SOL, teacher grading policies, school attendance, getting academic help, and grade level progression.

The main purpose of parent involvement is to be consistent and to aim for a relationship with the teacher. Talk to parents with many details as to how you can make this relationship work. You must approach with the appropriate academic objectives. The parents should let their child know if they are opposed to something that shows a negative academic performance.

Teachers' procedures and assessments of how well their students are performing should be reintegrated each year also with the parent. More importantly, if their accomplishments were better than the previous progress report, make a note for each student.

The special and remarkable scores need recognition, not just for you, but procedurally to the parent. Sometimes, waiting until report card time is not a good strategy. Why not make a call home to the mom or invite her in for a brief conference? Each child needs the opportunity to establish techniques to accomplish a good academic performance.

If parents do not know exactly what objectives are being accomplished having a meeting with the teacher let us discuss it? Establishing a good relationship with the parent makes it easier for you to work with your students. When I was teaching, it was a good idea, which you mention to the student, that you were going to call their parents.

If there was any behavior modification for this particular student, letting him know in advance is most helpful. In many cases, if the parents do not come to you, think about going to their home to establish a relationship. Then you can always invite them into the classroom at a later date. The impact this will have on the parent will help support and lead to continuous parent participation.

Parents essentially are looking for a dedicated, understanding, and genuine teacher that shows concern and commitment to their child. Teachers should give every opportunity to make the parents encouraged about being a part of the class.

If you can demonstrate consistent collaboration with the parent, then this will lead to great effects with the student also. Let us hope to see more of establishing many of the ideas listed because it leads to student academic achievement. In order for the child to accomplish this, there should be a contract made between parent, teacher, and child.

Parent/Educational Meeting at a Different Location

It was brought to my attention by my husband that we should set up a meeting with this nearby complex to spread our message to parents that lived there. Some of the people that lived in the complex had children that were students in our school district. Most of the parents did not know about our committee, so having this meeting was a good way to introduce the group and to meet the principals together.

We decided to call this meeting Meet the Principals Night. The principals were the presenters of WJC schools. My husband and I checked out the area more closely and talked with some of the residents. It seemed like a difficult situation because we only met a few people during our visit. Ultimately, our committee agreed to put on this event.

We contacted as many principals as possible, and we received confirmations of six administrators. As the committee prepared for this event, we thought about how many parents would come. Our committee was very appreciative that the main office team of the apartment complex had given us permission to have our event there. This team at the office, who also believed in the work of our group, had accomplished working with parents.

We had a parent /education event in a different kind of setting. This was not a usual location. This is evidence that the PCSCC will approach places that were out of the norm to recruit parent involvement. What an appropriate accomplishment to promote Parent Community School Connecting Committee and, at the same time, hopefully get other parents involved also.

The principals were very satisfied with the recognition they received, and this particular development was contact many times before. The involvement with parents was a critical problem with some of the parents that lived there.

There were many negotiations but very few parents followed through with a commitment. That evening event was set up for 7:00 p.m. The principals did a great job presenting an explanation speech about what services were offered at their schools to benefit parents and students. Parent attendance included six parents, but every parent you can reach has an impact.

The PCSCC has often expressed that you can't persuade every parent to become involved. But our approach to conducting this event was important. At least, the parents that live in this complex knew about our committee and the services offered by the principals at their schools. Everything that was presented is essential information that parents need to be provided with as often as the opportunity presents itself.

Chapter 8

The Parent Community School Connection Committee took the responsibility of promoting parents to get involved with their child's education. We found it necessary to advocate parents to fulfill this concept. Our responsibility was to empower parents to join our committee and start going to the school to meet their child's teacher.

This kind of advocacy is essential for the parents to understand a relationship with their child's teacher is critical in order to promote academic achievement for their children.

This particular objective to help our minority students is a difficult situation, but if the teacher and parent make a contract to acknowledge their relationship, there will be success.

Many studies have stated that the only way to close the minority achievement gap is to recruit the parents. Our committee took the opportunity to work diligently to get those parents to visit the school. The PCSCC was motivated and dedicated to make an impact on this theory. Everyone on the committee truly and genuinely believed that parent participation is a necessary part of the school system. This is a way of decreasing the academic achievement gap. Most of the scores previously were much higher. This means a wider achievement gap, but smaller numbers mean that the gap has decreased. It is an advantage for the minorities. This must continue on this track. The implication is that when parents are involved, the children do better in everything. Our members genuinely believed this concept and displayed the initiative to establish and develop strategies that would prove successful, and the Sols were cut to half. To be able to see these results makes all your time, energy, and dedication worthwhile.

The results of the achievement gaps in math are trending correctly in the JCC public schools. The Sols from a long term study. It shows that improvements were made by the minorities. Majority compared to Minority measured 30 points. The minority and majority students' gap decreased significantly—from *thirty-point difference down to thirteen points*—which is a tremendous drop in the minority achievement gap. These achievement scores have improved in recent years. These charts are just to give you an example of how effective parent involvement works. Now we must continue to keep parents going to the schools continually to keep their child's academic achievement at a higher level.

Chapter 9

Grading a Child is important

How do we evaluate a student? <u>Use the Formal and Informal evaluations</u>

By using the ultimate evaluation of a student which is two types of evaluations:

Informal

- Guided practice
- Rehearsal of learning
- Measured progress

Formal

- Achievements and accomplishments
- Report card grade
- Letter or percent grade

Deciding on a Grading System

- Evaluation—reflects student's ability
- Understanding—fair, balanced, doable for kids
- Simple—could be understood and is manageable

Balanced Grading

Fair—True

Population Dependent-

Supplied by the WJCC schools

Table 5. Classroom example of evaluating tests, classroom and report cards, all of each total 100%

Tests	40%	Nine Weeks 40%
Class work	30%	Nine Weeks 40%
Homework	30%	Exam 20% = Total 100%
	Total= 100%	Total Classroom weeks that school is in section.

This is divided quarterly for report card grading.

Key Messages for Kids

When you are in class, do the work.

Everyone starts out at 100 percent.

Late credit or some credit is better than zero credit.

Unless you have failed a nine weeks, exams do little to determine your grade unless you make perfect scores. Parents in the classroom with the teacher will improve academic enhancement. The Parent Community School Connections Committee was developed to encourage unengaged parents to get involved with their child's education. The reasoning for consistence reminding parents to get active, it is the only way for your child to grow in their class room achievements. As a teacher, I know it works because of my personal experiences in the classroom.

My conclusion and thoughts are, hopefully parents will pledge to increase their responsibility to help their children's academic achievements by working in the classroom on a regular basis.

Parents need to improve their techniques by making a contract or a relationship with the teacher. If both sit down and have a conversation, it will turn into a positive relationship.

If parents put more emphasis on commitment and working on classroom activities, their child's education scores will increase, and we can close the minority achievement gap. The PCSCC promotes the slogan, "We can help parent involvement one parent at a time."

Chapter 10

Note: All the statistical information on the students was gathered from the WJCC schools or from the Parent Community School Connections Committee. The work our committee displayed on parent involvement did increase the scores of the minority students.

Information collected from WJCC School System According to the Math Achievement Gap Trends

The achievements gaps in math are trending in the right direction for minorities, Hispanics, and majority students of the WJCC schools on the Virginia Standard of Learning (Sols). Significant improvement was made by majority students (+30 percentage points,) by Hispanic students (=15 percentage points increase)and minorities (+30 percentage points) from 2006 to 2010 in mathematics. The achievement gap in math between minorities and majorities students decreased significantly, a thirty-point difference down to a thirteen-point difference (-13.04) (AYP Data Source: NCLB). These are the scores that students aquired on their SOLS testing, which is a Federal testing procedure.(Under no Child Left Behind.)

The results from the testing that was conducted show great signs that the Minority gap had lowered tremendously. (Williamsburg James City County schools reports—testing took place 2006-2010. Our committee, the PCSCC, was working with parents to help close the achievement gap for minorities. During most of those years our committee was very active getting parents into the schools during—2006 to 2010. Our PCSCC was very excited about the performance of the students on their testing scores. Our membership of professionals assisted those parents and students. These members of the school staff on the Parent Community School Connections Committee deserve the credit for all their hard work and commitment to the parents and students.

The purpose of giving recommendations supporting parent involvement which is associated with the establishing good achievement motivations. The requirement for effectiveness and dedication will depend on parent participation. Parents can genuinely establish appropriate continued performance for the children just by taking the initiative to visit the classroom and talking to the teacher.

Parents need to persuade their children to gain the appropriate knowledge by listening closely to their teacher's classroom message. Consideration and true conceptions of the right approach from parents will improve academic performance.

Intensive responsibilities will help parent participation effects become stronger and consistent objectives and commitment to a parent and teacher partnership. Parents will need to successfully put all their emphasis on visiting the teacher and diligently working on activities in the classroom. Technology and procedure are essential to better classroom objectives for your child.

Parents, you have every opportunity which ultimate shows implication of success and enhancement in establishing and effective parent involvement consistency.

Our Parent Community School Connections Committee has made documented procedures as we recruited parents to be a part of their child's education. Many parents have stated our committee has given them more hope about the visit to their child's classroom. The group took information from this survey form that parents filled out. All the results and implications document evidence show that the PCSCC had much of the influence, persuasion, and recruitment of parents to get involved with their child's education. Parent Community School Connections Committee wants to continue working with parents and encourage them to visit the classroom. Parents believed in our committee and worked with us for about four and ½ years to build a relationship with the schools. Many of the parents were very comfortable working with our members.

This kind of partnership we developed was just what we used to convince the importance of maintaining an ongoing relationship with the PCSCC and the school systems.

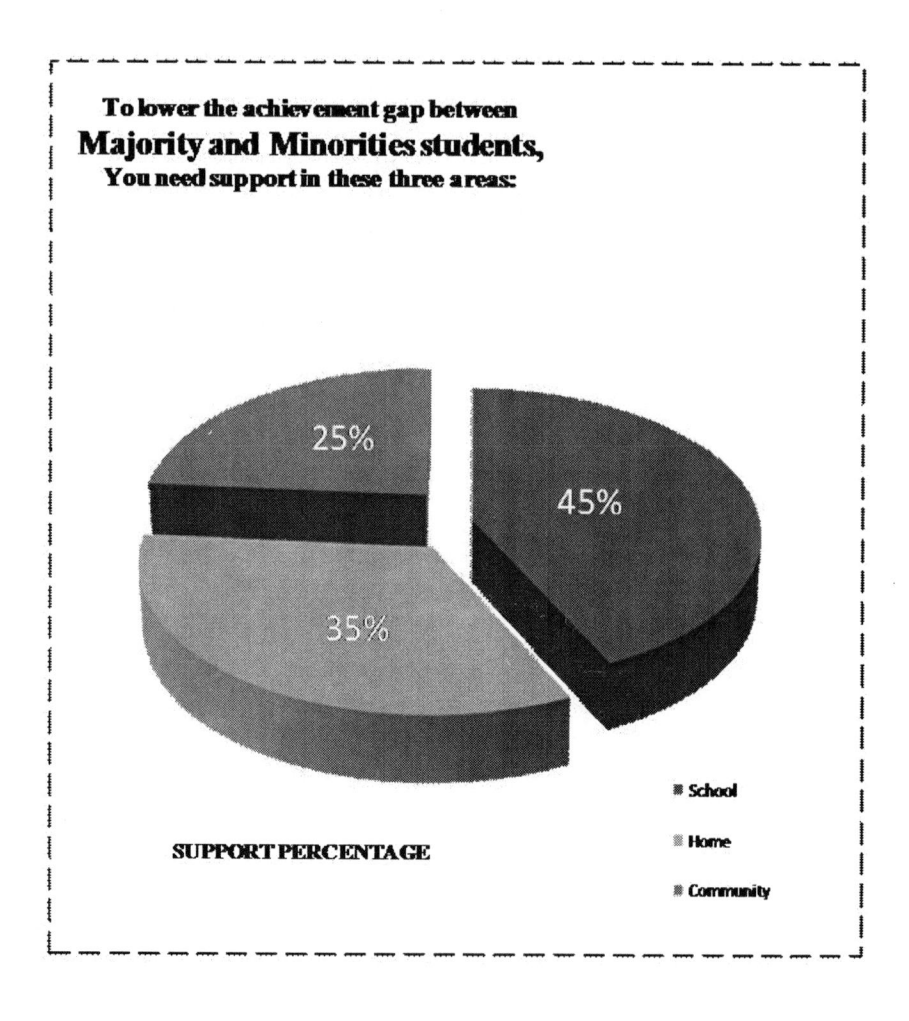

To lower the achievement gap between Majority and Minorities students, You need support in these three areas:

- School: 45%
- Home: 35%
- Community: 25%

SUPPORT PERCENTAGE

References

Callison, William L. Raising Test Scores, Using Parent Involvement, "Family-School Relationships." (1), pp 1-4

Ibid Carllison, "Importance of a Two Way Conversation," (2), pp 5-7

Ibid Carllison, "Parent Involvement Academic Performance." (2) p 2

DiLorenzo, Louis T. Which Way for Pre- K: wishes or reality, American Educations, 7, 1971, p30

Elementary School Journal. 1991. "School Programs and Teachers Practices of Parent Involvement in the Inner City Middle and Elementary Schools." *The Elementary School Journal* #91 (3): abstract.

Henderson, Anne, Berla, Nancy Ed., 1994. Parent Participation and Achievement, P 174

Jackson, B. L., and B. S. Cooper. "Involving Parents in Improving Urban Schools." *NASSP Bulletin* 76 (543): 30-38.

Karnes, Merle E. Jr., Immediate, Short term and Long-Range of five Preschool Programs for Disadvantaged Children, Ed. March, 1978- pp 043-152

Leach, D. J., and S. W. Siddall. 1990. *Parent Involvement in the Teachers of Reading* 60: 349-355.

Lindle, J. C. 1989. "What Do Parents Want from the Principals and Teachers?" *Educational Leadership* 47 (2): 12-14.

Moore. R. 1991. Improving Schools Through Parent Involvement, Principal, 71 (1): pp. 17-20

Pashler, Hal. PhD., 2007 September, Organizing Instruction and Study to Improve Student learning. "Teachers have to do more preparation in their classroom." "The best way is to recruit parents into your classroom." pp 1-4

Swap, S. M. 1990. "Comparing Three Philosophies of Home-School Collaboration." *Equity and Choice* 6 (3): 9-19.

US Department of Education. 1994. "Strong Families, Strong Schools: Building Community Partnerships for Learning." Ed. Publication No pp. 381-888 Washington, DC: US Government Printing Office.

Weisz, E., 1990. Developing Positive Staff-Parent Partnerships in High Schools. "American Secondary Education" 19 (1): 25-28

William, D. L., and N. F. Chavkin. "Essential Elements of Strong Parent Involvement Programs." *Educational Leadership* 47: 18-20.

CPSIA information can be obtained at www.ICGtesting.com
Printed in the USA
BVOW031400111112

305176BV00001B/85/P